百变上海

SHANGHAI NOW AND PAST

撰文　汤伟康
摄影　浮　图

上海人民美術出版社
SHANGHAI PEOPLE'S FINE ARTS PUBLISHING HOUSE

外滩全景，1925年 / A full view of the Bund, 1925

Photo by
CHUNG HWA
Shanghai

外滩全景，2014年 / A full view of the Bund, 2014

从浦西看浦东，1880年代 / *A view of Pudong from Puxi, 1880s*

从浦西看浦东，2018年 / A view of Pudong from Puxi, 2018

AURORA

百变上海

汤伟康

上海的魅力在于变。上海是个充满动感、变迁节拍快捷的城市。人口、商品、风尚、思想，乃至建筑、社区都在变，一个变字让上海这座城市充满无穷无尽的活力。100多年来，生活在这座城市里的人们不断追逐新鲜事物，着力塑造上海人所谓“海纳百川”的自信。

因为商务的关系，上海在19世纪末已建立起中国与欧美国家信息交换的枢纽。租界的辟设，使欧洲近代市政及管理制度一夜之间被移植到上海。近代生活方式，也因租界政府和侨民的极力推崇，让上海演变成世界著名的大都会。同是一个变字，让被世人讥讽为不伦不类、不中不西、亦中亦西的“洋泾浜文化”现象，从上世纪初开始，历经100多年，蜕变为今天人们津津乐道、引以为自豪的海派文化。这种兼容并包、与时俱进的文化现象，究其根源，就是华洋共居、五方杂处、中西结合、互相采纳的生存空间的内核裂变生成的。

日新月异的城市变迁使上海人一直在寻求一种留住记忆的方法和载体。犹如望远镜和显微镜是人类视力的延伸，电话和网络是语言的延续，犁耙和刀剑是手臂的延长，《百变上海》就是一本以摄影手段留住上海城市建筑时空变换的书籍。新旧建筑和城市风貌，被摄影家聚焦，留给世人的是对上海城市历史文脉的记忆与想象。

上海固然很少秦砖汉瓦的古建筑，但是历经100多年形成的近代都市氛围，却领先于全国其他城市。读者可以从《百变上海》中鉴赏到半个多世纪前和当今两代摄影家对同一座城市建筑的隔时空对话，这些建筑连同周遭语境所形成的城市文化环境和历史背景，充满了世界主义风格。

百变城市遭遇瞬间定格的摄影镜头，可谓动静相宜。每个人都有自己的城市，那个城市就是自己的灵魂。生活在上海这座向世界开放了160多年的城市里的人们历经时世变迁，中国人、西方人、本地人、外地人，在这100多年的交往中，已逐渐边缘不清，混为一种新型的城市市民——上海人，阿拉上海人正可通过《百变上海》来解读自己心灵中的这座城市。

SHANGHAI: NOW AND PAST

Tang Weikang

Shanghai's status as a glamorous metropolis in East Asia has benefited from a worldwide process of rapid urbanization since the late 19th century, in which the city has developed an impressive cityscape as well as a characteristic lifestyle.

The glamour of Shanghai comes from the constantly changing city itself. Shanghai has undergone significant fast-paced changes in its population, commerce, fashion, ideology, architecture, communities, etc. It is the changes that have led to the lively scene of the city. For over a century, the people of Shanghai have embraced new ways of life with a profound confidence that contributes to the city's eclectic character.

Thanks to its trade ties, Shanghai had already been a window of cultural exchanges between China and the Western countries by the end of the 19th century. The establishment of the foreigners' settlements (or Concessions) allowed the European systems of public services and municipal management to be installed in Shanghai almost instantly. When the modern lifestyle was introduced into Shanghai with foreign settlers, merchants and their extraterritorial government, Shanghai began to sport some noticeable cosmopolitan flavors, though it was often deprecated as a "pidgin" culture that belonged to neither the Chinese nor the foreign side. Since the beginning of the 20th century, Shanghai has developed into a highly eclectic culture on which its people pride themselves. It is worth noting that the culture of Shanghai has arisen from its unique historical situation that people coming from different places interact with and learn from each other, thus creating open and receptive mindsets.

The people of Shanghai are glad to find a means to maintain their remembrances of the city. *Shanghai: Now and Past* is a pictorial book to record the vicissitudes of Shanghai with photography. Buildings, roads, bridges, rivers, etc. – all these city scenes, old and new, help to rekindle people's memories of how the city was like and ignite their imaginations of in what ways Shanghai will develop in the future.

In the nationwide urbanization since the 1990s, Shanghai has also faced a problem of preserving its heritages, both material and intangible, amidst its rapid modernizing progress. Although Shanghai doesn't rank among the A-list historical cities of China, it does boast a considerable collection of heritage sites well surpassing most Chinese cities, thanks to its active role in the Chinese modern history. *Shanghai: Now and Past* presents an interesting duo of each of Shanghai's famous city scenes – one photo shot over half a century ago, and the other shot at the same site today. Such comparisons are like dialogues across time and give an insight into the cultural and historical backgrounds of the cosmopolitan city of Shanghai.

The constantly changing city is captured in the camera lens – that is quite an artistic rendering of the dynamic turning into stillness. For the people of Shanghai, regardless of their origins from other places or countries, they can all be called "Shanghainese" as they cherish the city which has been open to the world for 160 years. And is there a better way of depicting their city than with this pictorial book *Shanghai: Now and Past*?

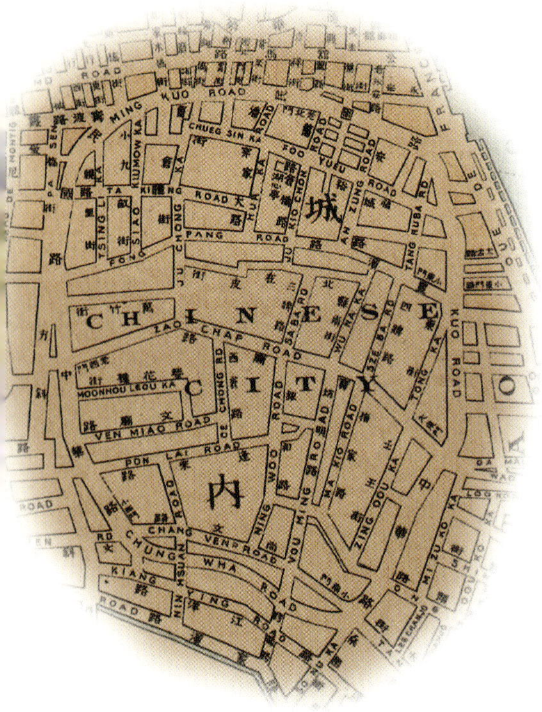

老城厢故事

元代至元二十九年，也就是1292年，上海正式设县，“上海县”成为一级地方行政机构，出现在元帝国的版图上，延续至今，有700多年了。人们对上海县城的认识，是以城墙为标志的。按照中国城市等级制度，县城可以修造城墙。但是，在建县后的261年中，上海没有建城墙，有点不像城市。建筑城墙的功能是防御兵匪。上海地处海滨，上海人看见兵匪是在明代以后。上海的富裕引来中国海盗和琉球倭寇合伙抢劫，他们多次呼啸而来，席卷财物而去。不得已，筑城墙。明嘉靖三十二年（1553年）建成长九里，高二丈四的城墙。墙外开濠，护城河水接通黄浦江、洋泾浜、泥城浜，通朝汐。城墙内的县城风景煞是好看，河上有桥，浜里有船，水是活水，城是青城。

上海老城厢也是个人物大家辈出的地方。声名最显赫的是明末崇祯年间任东阁大学士的徐光启。徐光启皈依天主教，虽位重一时，却对北京混乱的政治若即若离，他研究西方天文、历算和农业、水利、军事工程，业绩斐然。此外，还有一个不得不提的人就是建造豫园的潘允端。潘允端当四川布政使，聚财暴发，为“豫悦老亲”，给父亲造豫园。豫园建成于嘉靖三十八年（1559年），设计出于造园高手张南阳之手，占地70亩，园内不乏名石、名木，营造格局巧夺天工。

上海也按礼制的规定供奉自己的城隍神。上海人选定的城隍老爷是宋代大词人秦观的七世孙，祖籍扬州的上海大名士秦裕伯。秦裕伯学问好，为人忠孝，办事能力强，明太祖朱元璋要他出来帮助治国平天下。秦先生坚守节操“一臣不事二主”。当他在洪武六年（1373年）死的时候，朱元璋说：“生不为我臣，死当卫吾土。”遂发谕旨，请他的灵魂做上海的城隍老爷。朱元璋杀臣如麻，此举为雅事，也可见秦裕伯的确非同一般上海人。后来的史实证明，秦裕伯这个城隍老爷确实有“灵”，上海在明代以后日渐发达起来。

老城厢城墙建成300年后，上海进入了大规模的工业化、城市化时期，商业、工业、人口过度发达，南市、北市相互沟通，不断有人要求拆掉城墙。1911年，革命党人一声令下，城墙被拆掉。然而，工商业北移的势头并没有改变原先中国一流的工商城市，老城厢反而落成了三流的居民社区，南市的现代工商业步步落后，反而是靠豫园、城隍庙、文庙、十六铺等传统特色产业站稳了脚跟，在上海形形色色的社区里占有一席之地，这样的局面一直维持了大半个世纪。21世纪后，南市老城厢社区在上海改革开放的大背景下不断催生出新的事物，城市风貌也同上海其他社区一起日新月异，日趋璀璨。

THE STORIES OF THE OLD TOWN

Shanghai as a Chinese administrative region has a history of over 700 years. In 1292 (the Yuan Dynasty), the county of Shanghai was officially established. Chinese county towns usually had town walls, but Shanghai had no walls whatsoever for 261 years after its establishment. In the Ming Dynasty, the coastal town of Shanghai began to suffer from pirate raids. Pirates from China and Wokou from the Ryukyu Islands often ransacked the rich town and got away in a hurry. Walls had to be built for protection. In 1553, a ring of walls, with a perimeter of 4.5 kilometers and a height of 8 meters, was built around Shanghai. The walls even had a moat, which was connected with Huangpu River and minor streams like Yangjingbang and Nichengbang. It was quite a beautiful sight inside the walls: boats scurried to and fro on the mildly flowing river past various kinds of bridges, and the town itself was covered in green foliage. The area enclosed in the walls became what is known as "the Old Town" today.

The Old Town of Shanghai is home to some big names in the Chinese history. The most famous person might be Xu Guangqi (or Paul Hsu, 1562 – 1633). Though a high-ranking official in the Imperial Academy, Xu converted to Catholicism and stayed away from the chaotic politics of Beijing. He helped to introduce Western astronomy and mathematics into China and achieved great success in agriculture, water conservancy projects and military affairs. Another well-known person is Pan Yunduan, a rich official born in Shanghai and working in Sichuan. Pan built a garden "for the pleasure of his aged parents", hence the name "Yuyuan", or "the garden of pleasure". The Yuyuan Garden was completed in 1559 and had a total area of 5 hectares, filled with all kinds of rare plants and exotic rockeries planned out by the most skillful craftsmen at the time.

According to the feudal rites, the town of Shanghai had its own Town God – Qin Yubo, a well-known scholar and local gentleman. Qin first served the Yuan Dynasty. After the fall of the Yuan Dynasty, Qin refused to serve the subsequent Ming Dynasty as he was afraid that his moral integrity might be compromised, even when Zhu Yuanzhang, the first Ming emperor, personally invited him to be a Ming official. When Qin died in 1373, Zhu Yuanzhang ordered that Qin be a holy guardian for the Ming Dynasty. Therefore, Qin was apotheosized as the Town God of Shanghai posthumously. Perhaps the Town God used his "magic" in blessing his people, as Shanghai thrived since the Ming Dynasty.

300 years after the completion of its walls, Shanghai began to see large-scale industrialization and urbanization; its commerce prospered, its industries boomed, its population exploded, and its northern and southern parts needed better connection. There were a lot of public appeals to pull down the walls. In 1911, at the order of the revolutionaries, the walls were removed and replaced with roads. As a result, Shanghai's industries moved to the northern parts and the Old Town became a backward residential area in the south lagging behind in the city's modernization. On the other hand, traditional businesses around the Yuyuan Garden, the Town God's Temple, the Confucian Temple and the Shiliupu Dock remained strong to serve the local residents. This situation lasted in the 20th century. In the 21st century, the Old Town sees a revival of its attractions in the all-round development of Shanghai.

豫园湖心亭九曲桥，1859年 / The Zigzag Bridge and the Lake-center Pavilion, 1859

豫园湖心亭九曲桥，2010年 / The Zigzag Bridge and the Lake-center Pavilion, 2018

老城隍庙，1860年代 / Town God's Temple,1860s

老城隍庙，2005年 / *Town God's Temple, 2005*

文庙魁星阁，1860年代 / *The Pavilion of Literary Talent in the Confucian Temple of Shanghai, 1860s*

文庙魁星阁，2011年 / The Pavilion of Literary Talent in the Confucian Temple of Shanghai, 2011

文庙，1860年代 / *The Confucian Temple of Shanghai, 1860s*

文庙，2010年 / The Confucian Temple of Shanghai, 2010

小东门，1860年代 / *The East Gate, 1860s*

东门广场，2010年 / The East Gate Square, 2011

大境关帝庙，1860年代 / *The temple of Guan Yu in Dajing, Shanghai, 1860s*

大境阁，2010年 / The Dajing Pavilion, 2010

新北门，1900年代 / New North Gate, *1900s*

丽水路北端，2011年 / The northern end of Lishui Road, 2011

小南门救火会钟楼，1930年代 / *The bell tower of the fire station on the Minor South Gate, 1930s*

中华路小南门，2011年 / The area of the Minor South Gate on Zhonghua Road, 2011

中华路邮电局，1920年代 / Telephone office on Zhonghua Road, 1920s

中华路邮电局，2011年 / Post office on Zhonghua Road, 2011

老西门红房子妇科医院，1884年 / *The "Red House" Gynecology Hospital near the Old West Gate, 1884*

老西门红房子妇科医院，2011年 / The "Red House" Gynecology Hospital near the Old West Gate, 2011

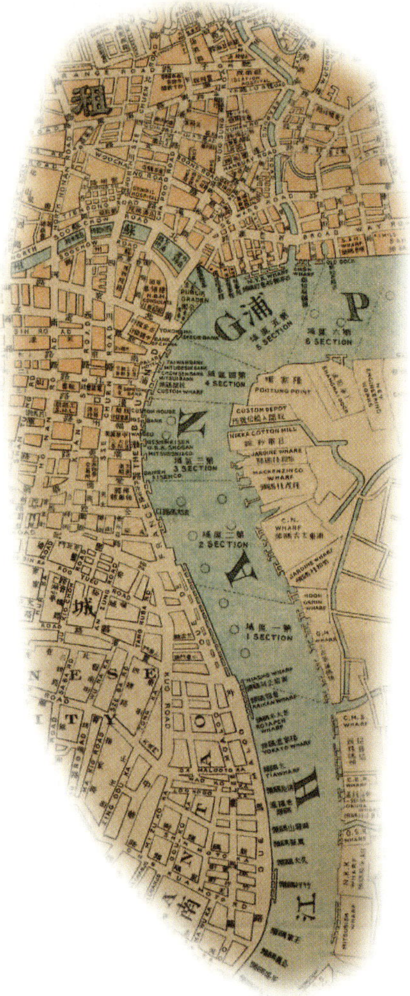

外滩 苏州河溯源

20世纪中西混杂的近代上海历史，是从外滩起源的。开埠初，外滩只是上海县城北面的一片荒滩，处于苏州河和黄浦江交汇之地。1845年，首任驻上海英国领事巴富尔凭借《土地章程》强租这块滩地。以后只用了半个世纪，外滩成了烟尘冲天、车马喧嚣的大卖场，成了后来上海“十里洋场”的起点。

外滩是一个富有象征意义的地方，各国领事馆大多设在这里，向人们显示着他们对这个城市的影响。外滩地位的重要，必然使之充满了政治性，租界重要的仪式都在这里举行。各式各样的人都曾希望用自己的历史观来讲述关于外滩和上海的故事，所以，外滩的纪念碑、塑像不断被矗立、推倒。相对于其他地方，外滩的西化景象更为纯粹，西方的文化、娱乐、生活方式比较彻底地在外滩展现。外滩的主人们都是暴发户，可是他们营造的大楼却力求贵族气派。大班们不惜巨资，不断地建造巨厦，来装饰外滩的门面。20世纪20年代，外滩变成了一片欧洲以外最欧洲化的街区。随着外滩建筑轮廓线的渐渐升高，一个生气勃勃的城市，向水平和垂直方向伸展。21世纪初，经过两次改造的新外滩充满生机，昔日有“万国建筑博览”的外滩建筑群在车流、人流分道，黄浦江畔空间大幅拓宽的江景烘托下提升出从未有过的精神与魅力。

外滩与苏州河紧密相邻。苏州河有两个名字：下游称苏州河，上游称吴淞江。在古代和近代上海历史上，吴淞江和苏州河是远比黄浦江更重要的河流。确切地说，苏州河才是上海的母亲河。苏州河的重要之处在于，它是联通富庶的江南地区和上海海上贸易的通道。苏州河两岸，有蜿蜒的马路，这些马路是上海发展的见证。许多上海市民原是从江南鱼米之乡进入上海，转为近代城市市民的。苏州河的历史，最鲜明地写在一座座大桥上。1907年，租界工部局用税收建造的外白渡桥是苏州河上所有桥梁的登峰造极之作。20世纪，上海开始成为世界上一个重要的工业城市。大量的修造船、面粉、棉纺织、丝织、机器制造、水电煤气、冶金工厂出现在苏州河、黄浦江沿岸，这些产业给上海带来巨大财富，也留下难以计数的污染。苏州河变得喧闹、污浊。早期的苏州河曾经拥有宁静的田园风光，蜿蜒的河流、清澈的水质。清同治《上海县志》评定当时上海最美的景致“沪城八景”，全是与苏州河、黄浦江有关的景点：海天旭日、黄浦秋涛、龙华晚钟、吴淞烟雨、石没月色、凤楼远眺、江皋霁雪。21世纪始，苏州河经多年的着力疏浚，再度显现当年风貌。随着岁月的推移，上海母亲河将再次焕发青春，与日新月异的上海城市面貌交相辉映。

THE ORIGIN OF THE BUND AND SUZHOU CREEK

The exciting history of Shanghai in the 20th century began with the appearance of the Bund. The place now called "the Bund" was originally a barren beach to the north of the Old Town, near the estuary of Suzhou Creek into Huangpu River. George Balfour, the first British consul in Shanghai, took this land by signing Shanghai Land Regulations with the local magistrate. In less than 50 years, the land became a highly popular business district of the foreigners' settlements of Shanghai.

The Bund is a symbolic place. The Western powers built their consulates there in an effort to showcase their influence on the city. The importance of the Bund was fundamentally political, as most of the major ceremonies of the Concessions were held there. People from different communities felt an urge to tell their own versions of stories about the Bund and Shanghai; therefore, the Bund saw a succession of statues being erected and destroyed. Compared with other parts of Shanghai, the Bund was more westernized in cityscape, culture, entertainment and lifestyle. A bunch of nouveaux-riches built their mansions on the Bund, yet they want the architecture to be as aristocratic as possible. Those "taipans" spared no efforts or funds to build most magnificent and impressive mansions on the Bund to rival against each other. As a result, the Bund had become the most "Europeanized" place outside Europe by the 1920s and its buildings kept rising higher and higher. In general the Bund has been widely seen as an epitome of the lively city of Shanghai. In the beginning of the 21st century, the Bund shines with rediscovered glamour after two thorough renovation project: now the traffic is more sensibly arranged and the waterfront space has been significantly expanded. The Bund boasts an attractive view that helps to set off its "showcase of world architecture".

The Bund is adjacent to Suzhou Creek, which is the downstream part of Wusong River. In ancient times, Suzhou Creek was much more important to Shanghai than Huangpu River and should therefore be called "Shanghai's mother river". The importance of Suzhou Creek lies in the fact that it linked the economically advanced regions in the Yangtze River Delta with the ocean-faring trade routes of Shanghai. A lot of people had left their hometowns in the Yangtze River Delta to settle permanently in Shanghai. The roads winding along Suzhou Creek and the bridges on it bear testimony to the history of Shanghai's development. The Garden Bridge, or better known as the Waibaidu Bridge in Chinese, was built by the Municipal Council (the governing body of the International Settlement) with tax revenue in 1907 and has been widely regarded as the culmination of all the bridges on Suzhou Creek due to its characteristic design. In the 20th century, Shanghai began to rise as an important industrial city, and a lot of shipyards, flour factories, cotton cloth and silk workshops, machinery plants, power plants, gas plants and metallurgic mills were founded near Suzhou Creek and Huangpu River. All these industrial facilities brought profits to the city but left heavy pollutions in Suzhou Creek. That is a big shame, considering that Suzhou Creek was once well-known for its idyllic scenery. In the "Eight Views of Shanghai" named in the late 19th century, most were related with Suzhou Creek. The 21st century has welcomed a restoration of Suzhou Creek's clear water and beautiful scenery after repeated dredging efforts. The mother river has been rejuvenated to match the exciting new looks of Shanghai.

苏州河、黄浦江交界处，1930年代 / *The estuary of Suzhou Creek into Huangpu River, 1930s*

苏州河、黄浦江交界处，2018年 / The estuary of Suzhou Creek into Huangpu Riverr, 2018

百老汇大厦远眺外滩，1940年代 / *A view of the Bund from the Broadway Mansion, 1940s*

上海大厦远眺外滩，2014年 / *A view of the Bund from the Shanghai Mansion, 2018*

外白渡桥苏州河口，1920年代 / *The Garden Bridge at the mouth of Suzhou Creek, 1920s*

外白渡桥苏州河口，2011年 / The Garden Bridge at the mouth of Suzhou Creek, 2011

外滩，1930年代 / The Bund, 1930s

第三次改造后的外滩，2018年 / The Bund after its third renovation, 2018

外滩十六铺码头，1930年代 / Shiliupu Port on the Bund, 1930s

改造后的十六铺码头，2011年 / *Shiliupu after renovation, 2011*

华懋饭店，1930年代 / Cathay Hotel, 1930s

和平饭店，2011年 / Peace Hotel (former Cathay Hotel), 2011

汇丰银行大楼与海关大楼，1930年代 / The building of HSBC (Hong Kong and Shanghai Banking Corporation) and the Customs House, 1930s

上海浦东发展银行和上海海关，2011年 / The building of Shanghai Pudong Development Bank and the Shanghai Customs, 2011

理查饭店，1930年代 / *The Astor House Hotel, 1930s*

浦江饭店，位于黄浦路15号，2011年 / *Pujiang Hotel, at No.15 Huangpu Road, 2011*

外滩公园，1940年代 / The Bund Park, 1940s

黄浦公园，2011年 / Huangpu Park, 2011

亚细亚大楼，1920年代 / *The Asiatic Building, 1920s*

中国太平洋保险公司，2011年 / The building of China Pacific Insurance Co., Ltd., 2011

外滩爱多亚路口，1920年代 / *The junction of Avenue Edward VII and the Bund, 1920s*

外滩延安东路口，2011年 / The intersection of the Bund Yan'an Road E., 2011

外滩爱多亚路口，1920年代 / The junction of Avenue Edward VII and the Bund, 1920s

外滩延安东路口，2018年 / The intersection of the Bund Yan'an Road E., 2018

洋泾浜，1900年代 / Yangjingbang Creek, 1900s

延安东路越江隧道口，2011年 / *Yan'an Road E. Tunnel across Huangpu River, 2011*

浦东远眺外滩，1920年代 / The Bund seen from Pudong, 1920s

浦东远眺外滩，2011年 / *A view of the Bund from Pudong, 2011*

苏州河下游鸟瞰，1934年 / *A bird's eye view of the downstream of Suzhou Creek, 1934*

苏州河下游鸟瞰，2011年 / A view of the downstream of Suzhou Creek, 2011

苏州河外白渡桥鸟瞰，1920年代 / *A bird's-eye view of the Garden Bridge, 1920s*

苏州河外白渡桥鸟瞰，2011年 / *A bird's-eye view of the Garden Bridge, 2011*

苏州河一景，1930年代 / *A view of Suzhou Creek, 1930s*

苏州河口外滩源，2011年 / The Bund Source in the south of Suzhou Creek, 2011

苏州河江西路桥，1930年代 / *The Jiangxi Road Bridge on Suzhou Creek, 1930s*

苏州河江西路段，2011年 / *Jiangxi Road near Suzhou Creek, 2011*

从上海邮政总局大楼西面远眺黄浦江，1930年代 / *A distant view of Huangpu River from the west of Shanghai General Post Office, 1930s*

从上海邮政总局大楼西面远眺黄浦江，2011年 / *A distant view of Huangpu River from the west of Shanghai General Post Office, 2011*

理查饭店和外白渡桥，1920年代 / The Astor House Hotel and the Garden Bridge, 1920s

浦江饭店和俄罗斯领事馆，2011年 / Pujiang Hotel and the Russian Consulate, 2011

乍浦路桥和光陆大楼，1930年代 / *Zhapu Road Bridge and Capitol Theatre, 1930s*

乍浦路桥和光陆大楼，2011年 / Zhapu Road Bridge and Capitol Theatre, 2011

百老汇大厦，1934年建成 / The Broadway Mansion, built in 1934

上海大厦，2011年 / The Shanghai Mansion, 2011

南苏州路，1920年代 / *South Suzhou Road, 1920s*

南苏州路，2011年 / South Suzhou Road, 2011

英国总领事馆，1873年建成 / *The British Consulate General, completed in 1873*

中山中一路33号，2011年 / No.33 Zhongshan No.1 Road, 2011

百老汇大厦和外白渡桥，1930年代 / *Broadway Mansion and Garden Bridge, 1930s*

上海大厦和外白渡桥，2013年 / *The Shanghai Mansion and Garden Bridge, 2013*

北外滩虹口码头，1910年代 / *The Hongkou dock of the Bund, 1910s*

北外滩国际邮轮码头，2014年 / *Shanghai International Cruise Terminal, 2014*

信号台和十六铺码头，1920年代 / *The signal tower and Shiliupu dock, 1920s*

信号台和浦江游船码头，2018年 / *The signal tower and Huangpu river cruise dock, 2018*

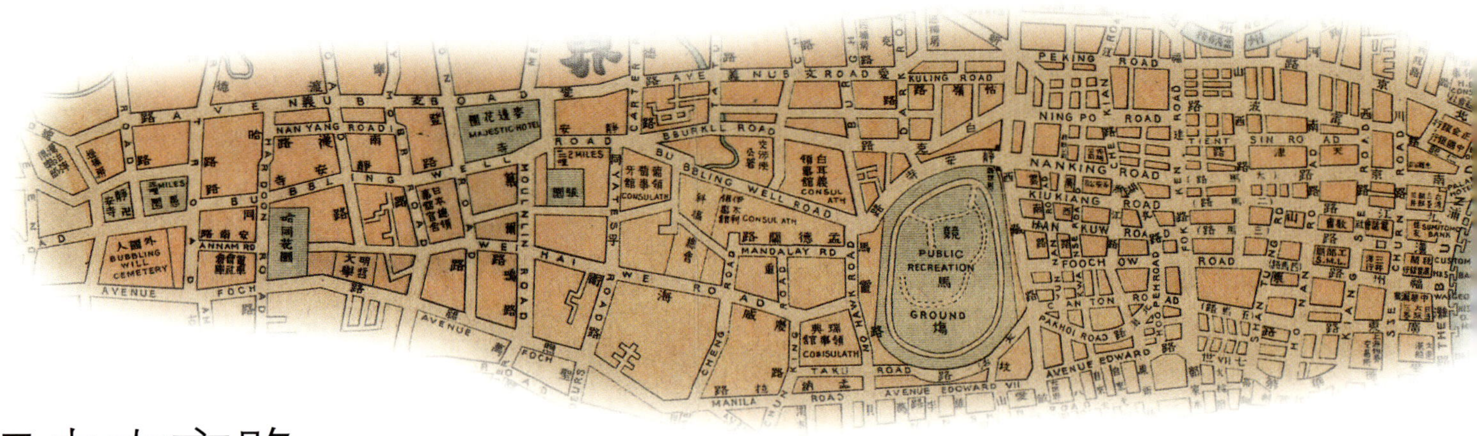

问史南京路

1865年，租界政府工部局正式命名公共租界里的首批马路，南京路列为第一，因此俗称“大马路”。南京路从20世纪初始，有流光溢彩的繁荣。这里马路最宽、商店最大、最洋派，已经先后取代了广东路、福州路，成为上海的商业中心。20世纪20年代，上海出售环球百货的四大公司，先施、永安、新新、大新公司，全部座落在南京路上。南京路执掌上海乃至全国商业之牛耳，历来被认为是中国商业精神的代表，现代生活方式的窗口。

南京路上点缀着中国式和西方式的不同建筑：在东头靠近外滩的部分，马路两边大多是西方式的大楼和营业场所。然而，从河南路往西，风景突变。横亘在这些大楼之下的是中国式的两三层本地小楼房。经营的是本土商业、娱乐业。所有商号都把市招和幌子挂到街中央，大拍卖、大减价的条幅连天接云。东西两向，土洋映照，对比强烈。南京路的“土”和外滩的“洋”，这种反差到今天还依稀可辩。

随着租界的西扩，公共租界的西部边界至1899年时已扩张至静安寺。静安寺路以寺庙得名，西自静安寺，东接南京路，静安寺路后改名南京西路。特别难得的是在上海城市化进程中，静安寺一带始终保持着一片田园般的境地。其优美之处，首先在于众多的园林，如张园、愚园、徐园、辛园、爱俪园、丽都花园、迪化公园等，还有历经沧桑的静安寺与静安寺对面的西人公墓陵园（今静安公园）相伴，舒适、空旷的生活空间时有上海滩“天堂乐土”之美誉。静安寺路的东端，则有远东第一高楼国际饭店，以及金门饭店等堪称精美绝伦的高层建筑，与外滩的万国建筑群遥相呼应。而在西区的中段，大量的公寓、新村建筑拔地而起，品质高档，内地军阀、官僚、大地主来此当“寓公”或用来“金屋藏娇”。随着大量中产阶级入住西区，一大批象征着上海20世纪水准的高档商店、娱乐场所沿路开设起来。卡尔登戏院（今新华电影院）、美琪、大都会、平安等高档影院，如群星璀灿般地衬托着当时最高级的大光明、大上海电影院，成了一大批标志性娱乐建筑，加上大华舞厅、维也纳花园舞厅、仙乐斯舞厅、百乐门舞厅为代表的上海滩四大舞厅，云集了专业舞女与酒吧。俄罗斯乐队、菲律宾乐队，夜夜笙歌，通宵达旦。21世纪的今天，这些具有标志性意义的建筑和场所，大多数被保存并使用，只是时过境迁，让人感叹。

THE HISTORY OF NANJING ROAD

Nanjing Road, as it is called today, was one of the first modern roads built in the International Settlement of Shanghai by the Municipal Council in 1865 and named "To Maloo" (the grand road) at the time. In the beginning of the 20th century, Nanjing Road became a popular shopping district featuring the city's biggest and most fashionable shops. Shanghai's four largest department stores in the 1920s, Sincere, Wing On, Sun Sun and The Sun, were all located on Nanjing Road. As a result, Nanjing Road has been recognized as a symbol of China's shopping business and a window of the modern lifestyle.

Historically, the different sections of Nanjing Road had different architectural styles and business models: there were mostly big, dignified mansions for banks and clubs in the Western style towards the Bund in the east, while small local businesses in low houses with two or three floors in the Chinese style could be found to the west of Henan Road sporting colorful placards and eye-catching "sale" signs. This contrast is still faintly visible in today's Nanjing Road.

By 1899, the International Settlement of Shanghai had expanded west to the Jing'an Temple, and Bubbling Well Road connecting the temple with Nanjing Road later became Nanjing Road W. In the early urbanization of Shanghai, Bubbling Well Road was an idyllic residential community with a lot of beautiful private gardens such as the Innocent's Garden, the Zhang Family's Garden, the Xu Family's Garden, the Tihwa Garden and the Hardoon Garden, as well as the picturesque Foreigners' Cemetery (now Jing'an Park) next to the ancient Jing'an Temple. The place was even praised as "Shanghai's heaven" for its desirable environments. In the east of Bubbling Well Road there were tall buildings like the Park Hotel, which took the top point of Shanghai for quite some time, and exquisite hotels like the Golden Gate, all corresponding to the magnificent mansions on the Bund. The middle section of the road, on the other hand, abounded with luxurious apartment buildings and villas which were owned by generals, high officials and landlords from inland. The wealthy residents on Bubbling Well Road frequented a collection of high-end shops and entertainment venues there, such as the Carlton Theatre (now Xinhua Cinema), the Majestic Theatre, the Metropolitan Theatre, the Empire Theatre and Shanghai's top cinemas – the Grand Theatre and the Great Shanghai Theatre. Professional dancing girls catered to clumsy customers to the music of Russian and Philippine bands in the city's four largest ballrooms – the Majestic Hall, the Vienna Garden, the Ciro's Dancing Palace and the Paramount Hall. Today, most of the old entertainment venues on Nanjing Road W. have been preserved as historical landmarks and some are still in use, yet it is their timeless charms that draw a continuous stream of nostalgic visitors.

汇中饭店，1908年建成 / The Palace Hotel, built in 1908

和平饭店南楼，2009年 / The south wing of the Peace Hotel, 2009

南京路，1920年代 / Nanking Road, 1920s

南京东路，2011年 / Nanjing Road E., 2011

圣三一教堂，1893年建成 / The Holy Trinity Church, completed in 1893

圣三一教堂，2011年 / The Holy Trinity Church, 2011

南京东路福建路口，1920年代 / *The intersection of Nanjing Road E. and Fujian Road, 1920s*

南京东路福建路口，2011年 / The intersection of Nanjing Road E. and Fujian Road, 2011

南京东路四大公司，1930年代 / *The four largest department stores on Nanking Road, 1930s*

南京东路世纪广场，2010年 / The Century Square on Nanjing Road E., 2010

先施公司和永安公司，1920年代 / Sincere Co. and Wing On Co., 1920s

上海时装公司和永安百货公司，2010年 / *Shanghai Fashion Co. and Yong'an Department Store, 2010*

先施公司，1930年代 / The building of Sincere Co., 1930s

上海时装公司，2010年 / *Shanghai Fashion Co., 2010*

南京东路鸟瞰，1920年代 / *A bird's-eye view of Nanjing Road E., 1920s*

南京东路鸟瞰，2010年 / *A bird's-eye view of Nanjing Road E., 2010*

南京路鸟瞰，1930年代 / *A bird's eye view of Nanking Road, 1930s*

南京路鸟瞰，2011年 / A bird's eye view of Nanjing Road, 2011

南京东路永安新厦，1930年代 / The New Mansion of Wing On Co., 1930s

南京东路，2010年 / Nanjing Road E., 2010

南京大戏院，1930年建成 / Nanking Theatre built in 1930

上海音乐厅，2011年 / Shanghai Concert Hall, 2011

永安公司，1918年建成 / *Wing On Co., founded in 1918*

永安百货公司，2011年 / Yong'an Department Store, 2011

大新公司，1936年建成 / *The Sun Co., opening in 1936*

上海第一百货商店，2010年 / *Shanghai No.1 Department Store, 2010*

南京东路口西藏路口，1930年代 / *The intersection of Nanjing Road E. and Xizang Road M., 1930s*

南京东路口西藏路口，2010年 / *The intersection of Nanjing Road E. and Xizang Road M., 2010*

上海大马路，1920年代 / *To Maloo (now Nanjing Road E.), 1920s*

南京路步行街，2010年 / The pedestrian street of Nanjing Road E., 2010

南京东路荣昌祥西服号等商铺，1920年代 / Rong Chang Xiang Suit Shop on Nanjing Road E., 1920s

南京东路第一百货商店，2011年 / Shanghai No.1 Department Store on Nanjing Road E., 2011

南京路新世界游乐场，1930年代 / The New World Amusement Park on Nanjing Road, 1930s

新世界商城，2010年 / New World Shopping Center, 2010

跑马厅鸟瞰，1930年代 / *A bird's-eye view of the Horse Race Track, 1930s*

人民广场鸟瞰，2011年 / A bird's-eye view of the People's Square, 2011

上海大世界，1917年开张 / *Shanghai Great World, opening in 1917*

上海大世界，2010年 / *Shanghai Great World, 2010*

爱多亚路鸟瞰，1940年代 / *A bird's-eye view of Avenue Edward VII, 1940s*

延安中路人民广场鸟瞰，2011年 / *A bird's-eye view of Yan'an Road M. near the People's Square, 2011*

西藏中路福州路口，1940年代 / *The intersection of Xizang Road M. and Fuzhou Road, 1940s*

西藏中路福州路口，2011年 / The intersection of Xizang Road M. and Fuzhou Road, 2011

沐恩堂，1931年建成 / *The Moore Memorial Church, completed in 1931*

沐恩堂，2010年 / The Moore Memorial Church, 2010

国际饭店和大光明电影院，1930年代 / The Park Hotel and the Grand Theatre, 1930s

国际饭店和大光明电影院，2010年 / The Park Hotel and the Grand Theatre, 2010

南京路鸟瞰，1930年代 / A bird's-eye view of Nanjing Road, 1930s

南京路鸟瞰，2011年 / *A bird's eye view of Nanjing Road, 2011*

福州路，1930年代 / Fuzhou Road, 1930s

福州路，2011年 / Fuzhou Road, 2011

百乐门舞厅，1932年建成 / The Paramount Ballroom, completed in 1932

百乐门舞厅，2010年 / The Paramount Ballroom, 2010

静安寺，1880年代 / *Jing'an Temple, 1880s*

静安寺，2010年 / *Jing'an Temple, 2010*

大光明电影院，1930年代 / *Grand Theatre, 1930s*

大光明电影院，2013年 / Grand Theatre, 2013

静安寺路西人公墓，1920年代 / *The Foreigners' Cemetery on Bubbling Well Road, 1920s*

静安公园，2013年 / Jing'an Park, 2013

赫德路，1920年代 / Hart Road, 1920s

常德路，2013年 / Changde Road, 2013

上海跑马场和国际饭店，1930年代 / Racecourse and Park Hotel, 1930s

南京西路，2013年 / Nanjing Road W., 2013

大中华饭店，1930年代 / Greater China Hotel, 1930s

福州路、西藏路口，2013年 / Fuzhou Road & Xizang Road, 2013

静安寺路、石门路，1930年代 / Bubbling Well Road and Shimen Road, 1930s

南京西路、石门路，2014年 / Nanjing Road W. and Shimen Road, 2010

上海跑马厅，1930年代 / The Shanghai Race Club, 1930s

南京西路，2014年 / Nanjing Road W., 2014

中央捕房和美国总会，1920年代 / The Central Police Station and the American Club,1920s

福州路上海市国家安全局，2014年 / *Shanghai National Security Agency on Fuzhou Road, 2014*

虞洽卿路，1930年代 / *Yu Ya-ching Road, 1930s*

西藏中路，2014年 / *Xizang Road M. 2014*

南京路，1930年代 / Nanking road, 1930s

南京东路，2014年 / *Nanjing road E., 2014*

广西路，1930年代 / Guangxi road, 1930s

广西路，2014年 / Guangxi road, 2014

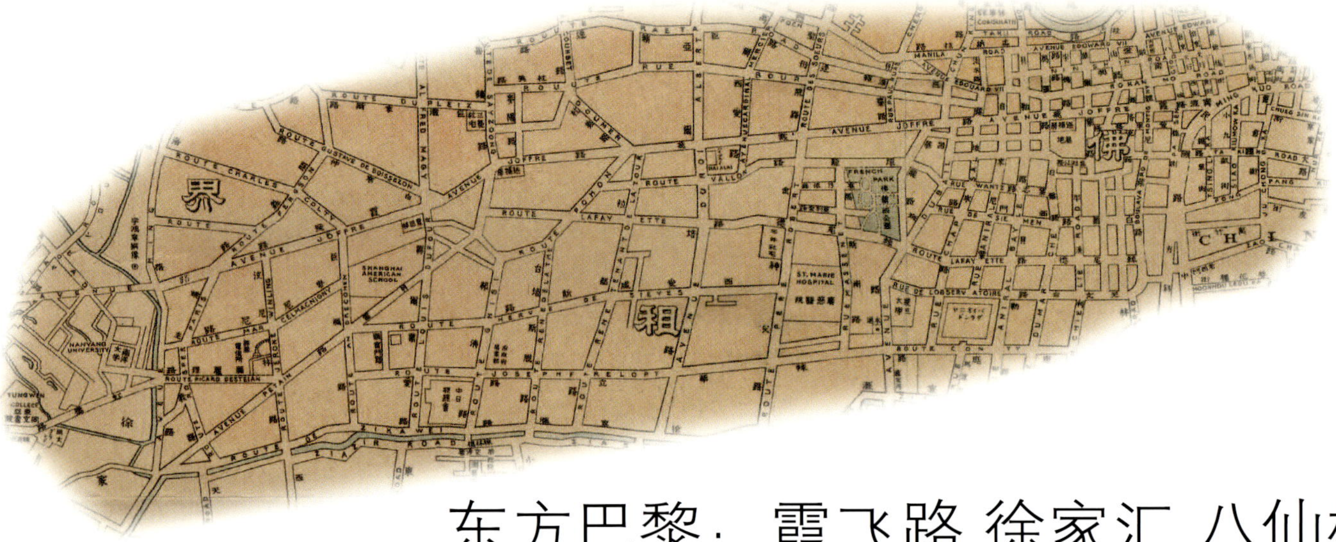

东方巴黎：霞飞路 徐家汇 八仙桥

人称“东方巴黎”的霞飞路（今淮海路），东起西藏路八仙桥，西通徐家汇，是法租界的核心地带。由于遇到了历史上少有的天时、地利、人和，这一地区在20世纪30年代发展成为上海最具魅力的国际化街区。霞飞路一带的商店，餐馆、酒吧、影院、公寓、别墅、新村，基本上消除了早期上海东部社区的本地化特色。这里的业主，大多采用欧洲建筑师的设计方案，用现代进口的建材，布置欧洲式的花园、橱窗。这里的街道，与欧洲的同期建筑风格比较接近。加上这里的居民结构非常国际化，欧洲裔人口主要集中在这里，加上混血的欧亚人，欧化的华人，霞飞路上自然到处是欧洲情调，异国风光。

20世纪20年代的上海，拥入了大批白俄难民，数额达十多万人，其中不乏俄国贵族、军人、商人、艺术家，还有大量受过良好教育、会说法语、多才多艺的俄罗斯姑娘给男女失调的侨民社会带来活力，减少犯罪，增加浪漫。果然，在霞飞路一带出现了许多西式的企业。霞飞路上的俄侨服装店，虽然没有南京路上的牌子老，但他们的款式、做工更接近欧洲风格。其他如面包店、咖啡馆、珠宝行、照相馆，经营的都是价廉物美的欧洲货。上海的欧洲生活方式，实际上是俄侨普及的，俄侨也为自己找到了坚实的谋生手段。以霞飞路为标志的法租界也是法国侨民聚居的地方。尽管在人数上法国人并不占优势，但法兰西的文化力量与生活方式吸引了许多国家的侨民入住本区。

从霞飞路西行，即可达徐家汇。徐家汇是天主教的重镇，这里有远东首屈一指的徐家汇天主堂。徐家汇教区直属法国巴黎耶稣会领导，传教的大多是法国神父，所以这里流传的是比霞飞路地段更纯正的法国文化。1897年，清朝大员盛宣怀创办南洋公学，也把校址设在徐家汇地区，进一步加强了徐家汇的文化气息。南洋公学凭国家扶助，发展成著名的交通大学，是中国“工程师的摇篮”。而近在霞飞路地区的震旦大学，也得力于耶稣会的严格训练，培养出中国最好的律师和医生。

霞飞路东端还有华洋交错的八仙桥地段（现大世界附近）。它的境内，既有差不多全盘西化的欧洲日常生活，又有典型的华人社会特征。法租界的国际化特色集中表现在徐家汇、霞飞路地区，而八仙桥附近的社会生活与上海华人关系密切，这里三界（法租界、华界、公共租界）地理交汇，社会生活方式十分奇特。

HUAIHAI ROAD AND "PARIS OF THE EAST"

People cannot talk about the Concession era of Shanghai without mentioning Avenue Joffré, a section of today's Huaihai Road from Baxianqiao in the east to Xujiahui in the west, which was the core zone of the French Concession. Thanks to a conjunction of favorable conditions, Avenue Joffré developed into a highly internationalized community in the 1930s. Shops, restaurants, bars, theatres, apartments, villas and residential areas near Avenue Joffré featured a modern international style that was significantly different from the traditional local flavors in the Old Town. Architectural plans and quality materials imported directly from European were used on European-style gardens and shop windows, and the street scenes looked pretty much the same as those in Europe. However, what made Avenue Joffré so Continental was its huge European population.

From the 1920s to the end of World War II, more than 100,000 Russian refugees came to settle down in Shanghai. They included Russian noblemen, soldiers, merchants and artists, not to mention that a lot of well-educated French-speaking Russian girls added a touch of romance to the expatriate community. This caused many European-style shops to appear on Avenue Joffré. The fashion shops owned by Russians, though not as prestigious as those on Nanjing Road, offered European designs in fine workmanship; bakeries, cafés, jewelry shops and photography studios all boasted authentic European styles. In a way, the Russian settlers had contributed to the modern lifestyle of Shanghai. In the French Concession represented by Avenue Joffré, the French population was actually not a majority, as people from different countries were attracted to the elegant environments of the Francophone culture.

In the west end of Avenue Joffré was Xujiahui, a well-known place of Roman Catholicism in China. St. Ignatius Cathedral, one of the grandest Catholic churches in the Far East, has remained till today. The parish of Xujiahui was run directly under the Paris-based Jesuit Society, and French missionaries served as priests in the churches of Xujiahui, so the place had an even stronger French influence than Avenue Joffré. Xujiahui was also overflowing with an academic aura, as an enlightened official Sheng Xuanhuai (1844 – 1916) helped to found Nanyang Public School in Xujiahui, which later developed into Shanghai Jiaotong University, "the cradle of Chinese engineers". Aurora University, founded by French Jesuits near Avenue Joffré, turned out some of China's best lawyers and physicians.

In the east end of Avenue Joffré was Baxianqiao (meaning "the Bridge of the Eight Immortals"), near today's Dashijie (Big World). The vicinity was a hodgepodge of foreign and Chinese lifestyles: modern influences of the French Concession near Xujiahui and Avenue Joffré, and traditional local folkways at Baxianqiao which was close to the Old Town. Baxianqiao featured a colorful mixture of different cultural scenes, as it was actually an intersection of the French Concession, the International Settlement of Shanghai, and the Chinese settlements.

淮海中路，1920年代 / Huaihai Road M., 1920s

淮海中路，2010年 / Huaihai Road M., 2010

淮海中路裴文公寓，1930年代 / The Bearn Apartment on Huaihai Road M., 1930s

淮海路裴文公寓和妇女儿童用品商店，2010年 / *The Bearn Apartment and the Women and Children's Shop on Huaihai Road M., 2010*

国泰大戏院，1930年代 / Cathay Theatre, 1930s

国泰电影院，2010年 / Cathay Theatre, 2010

淮海中路常熟路，1930年代 / The intersection of Huaihai Road M. and Changshu Road, 1930s

淮海中路常熟路，2011年 / *The intersection of Huaihai Road M. and Changshu Road, 2011*

常熟路，1930年代 / *Changshu Road, 1930s*

常熟路，2011年 / Changshu Road, 2011

淮海中路常熟路，1930年代 / *The intersection of Huaihai Road M. and Changshu Road, 1930s*

淮海中路常熟路，2011年 / The intersection of Huaihai Road M. and Changshu Road, 2011

淮海西路诺曼底公寓，1920年代 / *The Normandie Apartment on Huaihai Road W., 1920s*

武康大楼，2010年 / Wukang Building, 2010

新乐路俄罗斯圣母大教堂，1930年代 / The Orthodox Virgin Mary Cathedral on Xinle Roadl, 1930s

新乐路俄罗斯圣母大教堂，2011年 / The Orthodox Virgin Mary Cathedral on Xinle Road, 2011

圣依纳爵堂，建于1910年 / St. Ignatius Cathedral, built in 1910

徐家汇天主堂，2010年 / Xujiahui Cathedral, 2010

交通大学校门，1930年代 / The gate of Shanghai Jiaotong University, 1930s

交通大学校门，2010年 / *The gate of Shanghai Jiaotong University, 2010*

龙华庙会，1900年代 / Longhua Temple Fair, 1900s

龙华寺，2011年 / Longhua Temple, 2011

北四川路 虹口与江湾

以北四川路（今四川北路）为中心的社区，实际上是上海东区虹口的标志区域。这里的开发，始于1848年的美租界。后来，美租界与英租界合并为公共租界，注入了英国式的秩序，加上中国人的活力，这里在19、20世纪交替的时候开始发达起来。北四川路的零售业也是华人的天下，广东人集中居住在这里。20世纪20年代的粤菜中心，已从福州路转到武昌路，连带广式西餐馆也开办起来。其中如至今名声显赫的新雅粤菜馆，1927年创办在北四川路，后来迁至南京路。上海粤商大本营新亚大饭店，早在1934年即在此创办。

如果说北四川路是虹口地区的商业街区，与之匹配的虹口则是五方杂处的平民社会。虹口和美国教会关系深远，最早创设于美租界的美国圣公会主教文惠廉（William Bone，1811-1864年）的教堂就在虹口，昆山路景林堂一带有很多美国教会的财产。在上海传教的广东文昌人宋耀如全家曾住在这里。他在虹口办印刷厂，资助过穷困的革命家孙中山。他的太太青浦人倪氏桂珍，是徐光启家族的后裔。他们的子女是宋子文、子良、庆龄、蔼龄、美龄。宋家长期在景林堂做礼拜，宋美龄和蒋介石的教堂婚礼是由本堂的牧师主持的。民国时代，大量文学青年从内地、日本来到上海，大多喜欢有平民气息和日本风味的虹口，虹口成了作家成群的地方。鲁迅住在大陆银行建造的大陆新村，处于北四川路“越界筑路”的“半租界”。外国冒险家也来虹口凑市民生活热闹。虹口是中国最早的电影市场。沪上著名的虹口大戏院、维多利亚戏院、爱普庐戏院、爱伦戏院、上海大戏院、中国大戏院、沪江影戏院，都在以北四川路为核心的周边开设。虹口是日本人聚居的地方，这里有“小东京”之称。习惯于“五方杂处”的虹口居民，对日本人历来是容纳的。但当日本要鲸吞中国的时候，中国人也发怒了。日本人在虹口居住区内滋事以及虹口的抵制日货乃至抗日风潮一直没有停息过，直至1945年抗战胜利。

和虹口海宁路仅一路之隔的江湾曾经是华界的希望。1927年，国民党新政府决心开发江湾，企图抓住中国的经济命脉，雄心勃勃地实施“大上海建设计划”。然而，1932年的“一二八”淞沪抗战，1937年的“八一三”抗战，江湾成了北市的主战场，大都市被埋在荒芜的草丛中。尽管饱经风霜，屡遭废弃，但是一百多年建设现代化的努力，毕竟给后人留下不少遗物。

今天的虹口与江湾，面貌焕然一新，中国国际航运中心将在此建设，虹口与江湾成为大上海又一个中心城区。

HONGKOU AND JIANGWAN IN NORTH CITY

The development of Hongkou District in northeast Shanghai, centering on the core zone that is today's Sichuan Road N., began with the founding of the U.S. Concession in 1848. When the U.S. Concession merged with the British Concession to become the International Settlement of Shanghai at the turn of the century, the area began to thrive thanks to the British legislation and the Chinese diligence. Sichuan Road N. had predominantly Chinese-run retail businesses and became a favorite residential area of Cantonese people. By the 1920s, the center of Cantonese restaurant had shifted from Fuzhou Road to Wuchang Road near Sichuan Road N., and even Western-food restaurants in Cantonese styles appeared there. The famous Xinya Cantonese Restaurant was founded on Sichuan Road N. in 1927 and later moved to Nanjing Road. New Asia Hotel, a popular meeting place of Cantonese merchants in Shanghai, was founded on Sichuan Road N. in 1934.

Hongkou District had highly diversified civilian communities. The district featured a heavy influence of U.S. Christianity. The first U.S. church in Shanghai was founded by the U.S. Episopal bishop William Bone (1811 – 1864) in Hongkou. There were a lot of U.S. church properties near the Young John Allen Memorial Church on Kunshan Road, where Charles Jones Soong once lived with his family in the early 20th century. Charles Jones Soong, a Cantonese doing missionary work and running a printing business in Hongkou, supported Dr. Sun Yat-sen, then a financially stressed revolutionary, and reared his most famous offspring: T. V. Soong and the three sisters Soong Ai-ling, Soong Ching-ling and Soong May-ling. The Soong family made it a habit to attend the Masses in the Young John Allen Memorial Church, and a priest from the church officiated the wedding of Soong Mei-ling and Chiang Kai-shek. After the founding of the Republic of China in 1911, a lot of progressive-minded young people came to Shanghai from Chinese inland or Japan, and many writers chose to live in Hongkou for its affordable residence and Japanese ambience. For example, Lu Xun lived in the Continental New Village near Sichuan Road N. in the acquiesced expansion of the International Settlement of Shanghai. Westerners also liked to venture a taste of the Chinese folk life there. Hongkou District saw the earliest competitive market of cinemas in China, as there were Hongkou Grand Theatre, Victoria Theatre, Apollo Theatre, Allen Theatre, Shanghai Grand Theatre, etc., near Sichuan Road N. Hongkou was called "Little Tokyo" because it had a lot of Japanese residents. The Chinese people in Hongkou welcomed settlers from the world including Japan, but they became angry when Japan showed a clear intent of invading China. In fact, there were constant rallies of protest against Japanese merchandise and Japanese invasion in Hongkou until the end of World War II in 1945.

Jiangwan, a northern part of Hongkou, was once projected to be the hope of the Chinese districts in Shanghai. In 1927, the Kuomintang government made brilliant plans to develop Jiangwan in its "Great Shanghai Project" in order to revitalize China's economy. Unfortunately, in the wars against Japanese invasion breaking out on January 28, 1932 and August 13, 1937, Jiangwan became a battlefield in northern Shanghai, and the new constructions were either ruined or laid to waste. Some of the constructions at that time have been preserved as remainders of China's efforts toward modernization. Today, Jiangwan sports brand-new looks as the International Shipping Center of China is to be built there. Hongkou will be a new sub-center of Shanghai.

江湾老上海市政府大楼，1933年建成 / *The government building of Shanghai Special Municipality in Jiangwan, 1930s*

上海体育学院办公楼，2011年 / The office building of Shanghai Sports Institute, 2011

江湾原上海市博物馆，1933年建成 / The Old Shanghai Museum, built in 1933

长海医院影像楼，2011年 / *The radioactive filming centre of Changhai Hospital, 2011*

江湾体育场，1934年建成 / *Jiangwan Stadium, completed in 1934*

江湾休育场，2009年 / *Jiangwan Stadium, 2009*

东长治路，1930年代 / *Changzhi Road E., 1930s*

东长治路，2011年 / Changzhi Road E., 2011

三角地菜场，1860年形成菜市 / The Triangle Food Market, appearing in 1860

三角地菜场原址上的高楼，2011年 / *Skyscrapers on the former Triangle Food Market, 2011*

吴淞路，1930年代 / Wusong Road, 1930s

吴淞路，2011年 / Wusong Road, 2011

沪宁铁路上海老北站，1930年代 / The North Station of the railway from Shanghai to Nanjing, 1930s

上海铁路博物馆，2010年 / *Shanghai Railroad Museumi, 2010*

四川北路日本海军特别陆战队司令部大楼，1924年建成 / The Headquarters of the Special Corps of the Japanese Navy at the northern end of Sichuan Road N., built in 1924

四川北路多伦路口，2011年 / The intersection of Sichuan Road N. and Duolun Road, 2011

四川北路，1940年代 / *Sichuan Road N., 1940s*

四川北路，2010年 / Sichuan Road N., 2010

四川北路横浜路桥，1940年代 / *Hengbang Road Bridge on Sichuan Road N., 1940s*

四川北路横浜路桥，2011年 / *Hengbang Road Bridge on Sichuan Road N., 2011*

乍浦路虹口大戏院，1930年代 / Hongkou Grand Theatre on Zhapu Road, 1930s

位于乍浦路、江宁路口的虹口大戏院旧址，2014年 / The former site of Hongkou Grand Theatre at the corner of Zhapu Road and Jiangning Road, 2014

四川北路，1940年代 / Sichuan Road N., 1940s

四川北路，2010年 / Sichuan Road N., 2010

四川路桥北堍，1930年代 / The northern side of Sichuan Road Bridge, 1930s

四川路桥北堍，2011年 / The northern side of Sichuan Road Bridge, 2011

图书在版编目（CIP）数据

百变上海/浮图摄影 ；汤康伟编文. —上海：上海人民美术出版社，2018.6

ISBN 978-7-5586-0950-3

Ⅰ.①百… Ⅱ.①浮…②汤… Ⅲ. ①上海－概况－摄影集 Ⅳ.①K925.1-64

中国版本图书馆CIP数据核字（2018）第116794号

百变上海

本社编

撰　　文：汤伟康

翻　　译：梁瀚杰

摄　　影：浮　图

责任编辑：刘晓天

技术编辑：季　卫

装帧设计：信生工作室

出版发行：上海人民美術出版社

（上海长乐路672弄33号）

印　　刷：上海丽佳制版印刷有限公司

开　　本：889×1194　1/32　7印张

版　　次：2018年7月第1版

印　　次：2018年7月第1次

印　　数：0001-2300

书　　号：ISBN 978-7-5586-0950-3

定　　价：88.00元